Cambridge **Discovery Education**™

▶ **INTERACTIVE READERS**

Series editor: Bob Hastings

BRIGHT LIGHTS
ON BROADWAY
THEATERLAND

W0099612

A2+

Kathryn O'Dell

CAMBRIDGE UNIVERSITY PRESS
Cambridge, New York, Melbourne, Madrid, Cape Town,
Singapore, São Paulo, Delhi, Mexico City

Cambridge University Press
32 Avenue of the Americas, New York, NY 10013-2473, USA

www.cambridge.org
Information on this title: www.cambridge.org/9781107650220

© Cambridge University Press 2014

This publication is in copyright. Subject to statutory exception and to the provisions
of relevant collective licensing agreements, no reproduction of any part may take place
without the written permission of Cambridge University Press.

First published 2014

Printed in Hong Kong, China, by Golden Cup Printing Company Limited

A catalog record for this publication is available from the British Library.

Library of Congress Cataloging-in-Publication Data

O'Dell, Kathryn.
  Bright lights on Broadway : theaterland / Kathryn O'Dell.
      pages cm. -- (Cambridge discovery interactive readers)
    ISBN 978-1-107-65022-0 (pbk. : alk. paper)
  1. Broadway (New York, N.Y.)--Juvenile literature. 2. English language--Textbooks for foreign
speakers. 3. Readers (Elementary) I. Title.

F128.67.B7O44 2013
974.7'1--dc23

                                        2013023917

ISBN 978-1-107-65022-0

Additional resources for this publication at www.cambridge.org

Cambridge University Press has no responsibility for the persistence or
accuracy of URLs for external or third-party Internet Web sites referred to in
this publication and does not guarantee that any content on such Web sites is,
or will remain, accurate or appropriate.

Layout services, art direction, book design, and photo research: Q2ABillSMITH GROUP
Editorial services: Hyphen S.A.
Audio production: CityVox, New York
Video production: Q2ABillSMITH GROUP

Contents

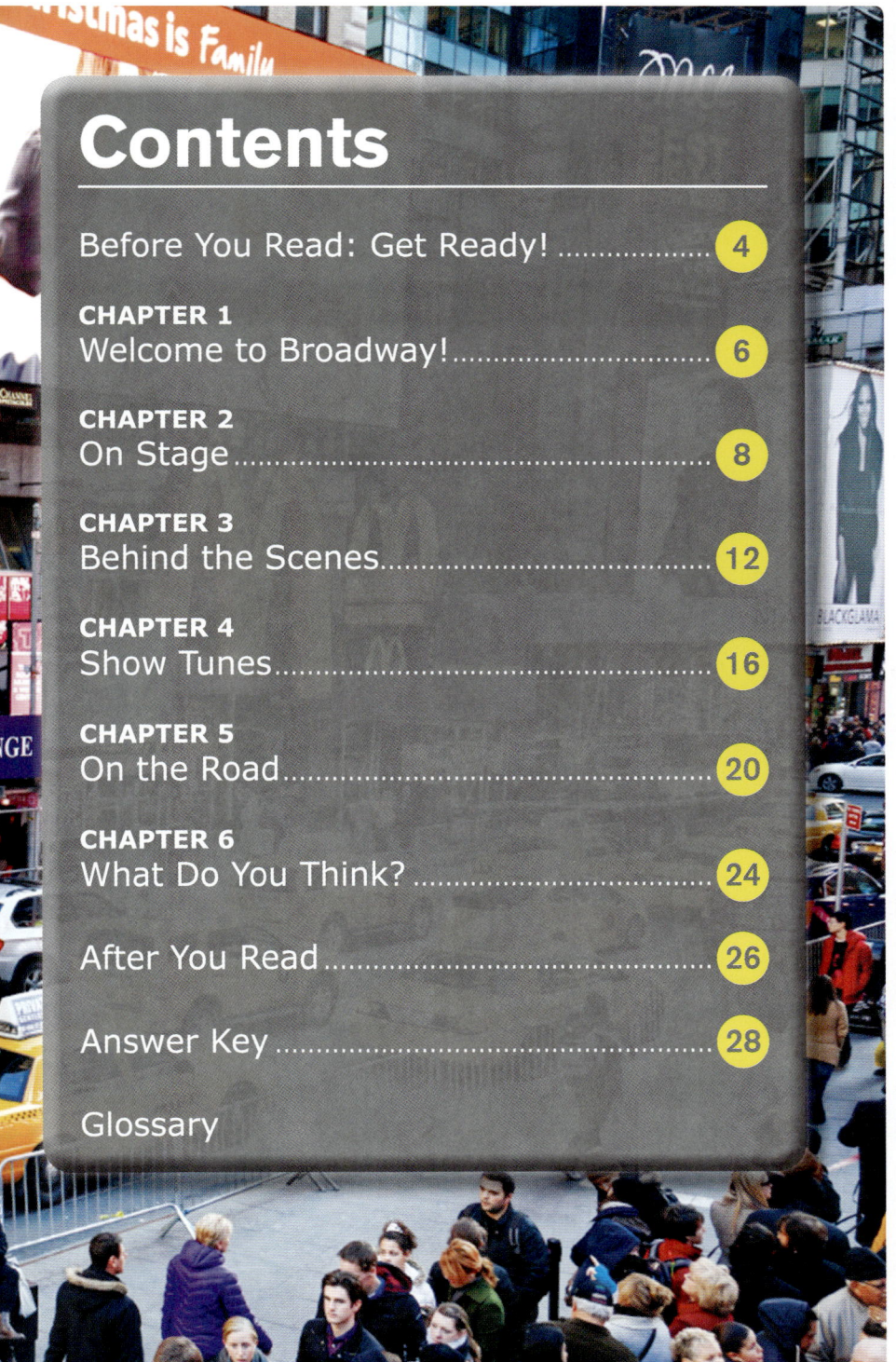

Before You Read:
Get Ready!

There is a lot of work that goes into making a Broadway show.

Words to Know

Read the sentences. Then complete the quotations with the highlighted words.

- The set includes everything on stage for a scene in a play. A scene is one part of a play. The set is the same in one scene, but it sometimes changes for other scenes. Things on stage to make the set look like a certain place are called scenery.
- The audience is the people who watch the play.
- A part is the person or animal an actor plays in a show.
- A musical is a play that also has music and singing.

"I play the ❶ _____ of Mufasa in the ❷ _____ *The Lion King*. My favorite thing about my job is making the ❸ _____ happy with my acting and singing." *–Tom Rollins, actor*

"My favorite ❹ _____ in *Spider-Man: Turn Off the Dark* is when Spider-Man flies in the air and catches the bad guys." *–Toby Bourne, 6*

"I work with ❺ _____ on *Mary Poppins*. I get the stage ready before the show." *–Josh Powell, stagehand*

"I love to create the ❻ _____ for a Broadway show. The hardest part is making it look real." *–Sandra Kim, set designer*

Words to Know

Read the sentences. Then label the photos with the highlighted words.

- A backdrop is a large piece of scenery at the back of the stage.

- A prop is a small piece of scenery that actors hold or carry.

- The props are kept backstage, behind the stage, until the actors need them.

- Actors wear costumes to make them look like other people or animals.

- Things sold at a Broadway play are called merchandise.

1 _____

2 _____

3 _____

4 _____

5 _____

In the early 1900s, white lights were used on Broadway.

CHAPTER 1

Welcome to Broadway!

WHAT IS A BROADWAY SHOW?

Toby is in New York City to see his first Broadway play. His eyes are wide as he walks through Times Square. He can't believe how many bright lights there are. Toby is only six, but older children and even adults have the same feeling. Times Square and the bright lights of Broadway can make anyone feel like an excited child.

New York City started having plays in the early 1700s, but the first big theater wasn't built until 1750. After the trains and subways were made in the late 1800s and early 1900s, plays became very popular in New York City. In 1891, theaters started using bright white lights to advertise[1] the plays. People called the area "The Great White Way" because the white light filled the streets.

[1] **advertise:** tell people about something on TV, on the Internet, or in a newspaper

Broadway got its name because in the past many theaters were on the street called Broadway. Today, there are only five theaters on the street, but there are about 40 Broadway theaters in the area. Today, a play is a Broadway show if the theater has seats for more than 500 people. An Off-Broadway theater usually has 99 to 499 seats, and most theaters in New York City with fewer than 99 seats are Off-Off-Broadway.

Toby is one of about 12 million people who see a Broadway play each year. The more people that go to a show, the more successful[2] it is. *The Phantom of the Opera* is the longest running Broadway play with over 10,000 shows. Some shows aren't as successful, and some even flop.[3] For example, in 1981, the play *Frankenstein* closed the same night it opened!

[2]**successful:** very popular
[3]**flop:** fail

?

ANALYZE
Why do you think theaters used white lights in the past? Why do they use colored lights today?

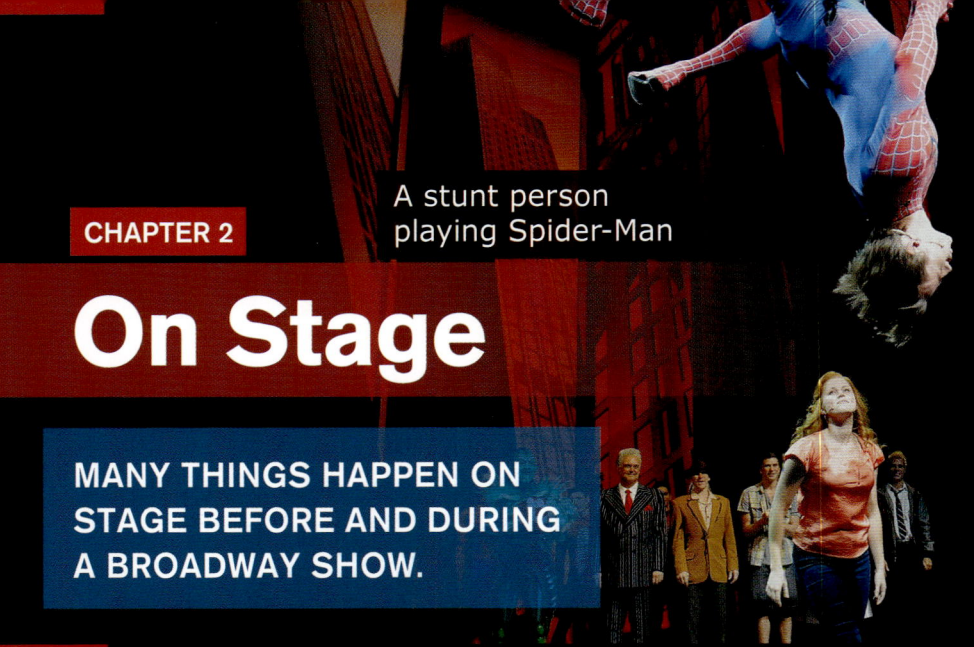

CHAPTER 2

A stunt person playing Spider-Man

On Stage

MANY THINGS HAPPEN ON STAGE BEFORE AND DURING A BROADWAY SHOW.

Toby sees *Spider-Man: Turn Off the Dark*. His Uncle Kevin is a **stagehand** on the show. After the play, Toby goes backstage for a surprise. Toby says, "When Kevin told me I might get to meet someone, I said, 'What? Who?' And it was Spider-Man!"

Toby knows the person he met is not really Spider-Man, but the **actor** who plays him. In fact, he didn't meet the actor who plays the main Spider-Man. It was the actor who plays Spider-Man flying through the air. In the play, eight actors play Spider-Man. Some of the actors are stunt people.[4] They fly in the air over the stage and over the audience. Toby was really happy to meet the actor. Many people wait after shows to meet actors and to get their autographs.[5]

[4] **stunt person:** an actor who does difficult and dangerous things, sometimes in place of the main actor

[5] **autograph:** a famous person's name written by that person

There are many different parts for actors on Broadway – big and small. Sometimes, an actor plays several small parts in the same play. Often, an actor has small parts or is in Off-Broadway and Off-Off-Broadway shows for years before making it big on Broadway.

For some parts, actors go to open auditions,[6] sometimes called "cattle calls" because hundreds of people, like a group of cows, wait for a turn. Some get called back to audition again, but only some of those actors get parts.

Others make it big quickly. Reeve Carney, who plays Peter Parker and Spider-Man in *Spider-Man: Turn Off the Dark*, was not an actor before he got the part. He was a singer and guitar player in a band when one of the writers and **directors** of the play discovered[7] him.

[6] **audition:** when several actors try to get a part in a play
[7] **discover:** find something or someone for the first time

Several actors play Spider-Man in the Broadway show.

Actors audition for a part.

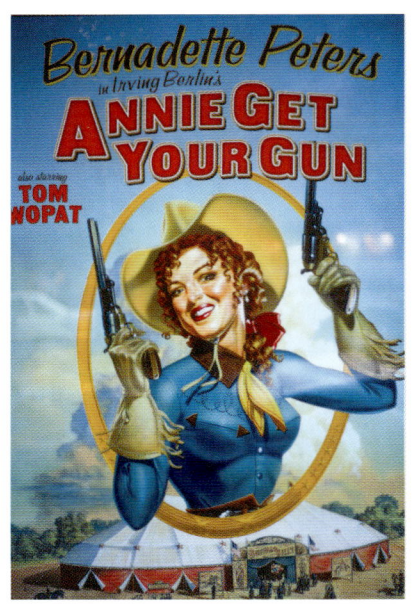

Bernadette Peters in
Annie Get Your Gun

Daniel Radcliffe in *How
to Succeed in Business
Without Really Trying*

Some actors prepare all of their lives to be in a Broadway show. They are called stage actors. Bernadette Peters is a stage actor who has starred in plays since 1959. Her first part was playing Tessie in the Off-Broadway show *The Most Happy Fella*. Two of her most famous Broadway parts were Annie Oakley in *Annie Get Your Gun* in 1999, and Sally Plummer in *Follies* in 2012.

Other actors start in movies and on television shows and then come to Broadway. Daniel Radcliffe became famous for playing Harry in the Harry Potter movies. In 2008, he was in his first Broadway show, and in 2011, he got the lead role[8] in *How to Succeed in Business Without Really Trying*.

[8] **lead role:** the main part in a play

Broadway actors rehearse – or practice – a play on stage for several months. They work with directors and coaches.[9] The director works with all of the actors to make all of the play go well. Coaches often help actors with certain things. For example, Daniel Radcliffe is from England and has a British accent.[10] In *How to Succeed in Business Without Really Trying* he plays an American. Language coaches often help actors learn to speak differently than they normally do.

Sometimes the writers of the plays are also directors and work on stage with the actors, and other times they are not. If a play has dancing in it, choreographers work with the actors to teach them the dances.

[9] **coach:** someone who gives lessons
[10] **accent:** the way a person speaks, showing where he or she comes from

Choreographers teach actors the dances.

Video Quest

The Actors

Watch this video to learn more about Broadway shows. What do actors do before they go on stage?

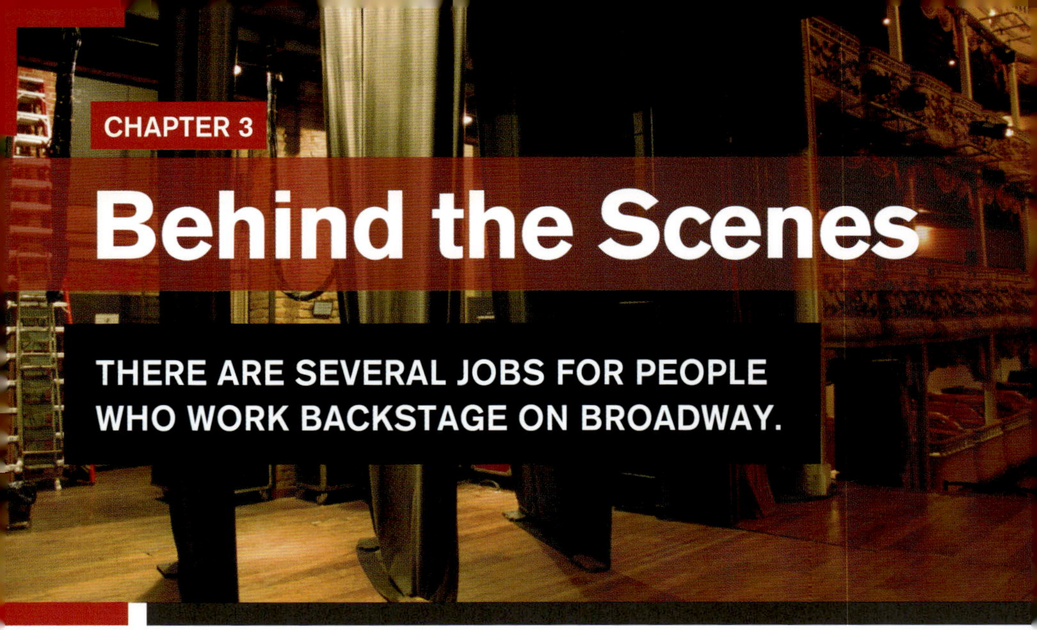

CHAPTER 3

Behind the Scenes

THERE ARE SEVERAL JOBS FOR PEOPLE WHO WORK BACKSTAGE ON BROADWAY.

Toby gets a backstage tour of *Spider-Man: Turn Off the Dark* from his Uncle Kevin. Kevin has been a stagehand on several Broadway shows, including *The Lion King* and *Mary Poppins*. For *Spider-Man*, he has many responsibilities.[11] Stagehands operate[12] the scenery that moves on the stage. In *Spider-Man*, there are a lot of props backstage and not much room, so parts of a car are kept backstage in the air. Before the scene, Kevin brings them down, and he puts the car together just before an actor drives it on stage.

Sometimes, stagehands move props onto the stage. Kevin says, "I wear black clothing when I'm on stage, so the audience doesn't see me."

A stagehand

[11] **responsibility:** something that is your job to do
[12] **operate:** make something work

There are many people who work behind the scenes months before a Broadway show starts.

The set in one scene from *Spider-Man: Turn Off the Dark*

Set **designers** create[13] the plans for the sets to change the stage into all kinds of places. They **design** large backdrops for each scene. For example, in *Spider-Man*, there are scenes at a school, in an office, and in a home. There is even a scene of New York City, where the audience feels like they are looking down at buildings and the street below.

The set designer also designs bigger props, like desks and furniture. Once the set designer creates the plan, artists and **carpenters** make different parts of the set. They paint backdrops, build furniture, and even make cars!

Once the set is ready, it is brought to the theater in pieces. Stagehands and carpenters put the sets together on stage.

[13] **create:** make something new

Video Quest

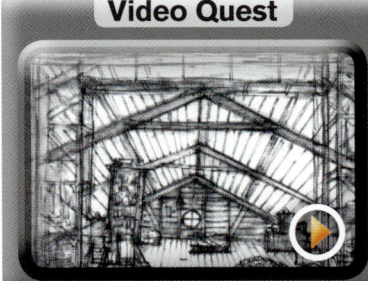

Set and Sound Designers

Watch this video to learn about these jobs. What does the set designer like about his job? What does the sound designer do?

Lighting designers also work for months before a show. They can use light to make the stage very bright, or they might have a dark stage with light on only one actor.

In 1975, Tharon Musser, a woman who worked on over 150 Broadway plays, changed the way lighting was used on Broadway. She was the first person to use a computerized light board. In the musical *A Chorus Line*, she used computers to design lights that changed faster and could quickly follow one actor dancing on stage.

Once the lighting is created, the lighting designer rehearses with the director and actors on stage. During the play, stagehands operate the lights. Some sit above the stage and shine bright spotlights on actors. Others sit in rooms at the back of the theater and use computers to turn lights on and off.

A computerized light board

A spotlight

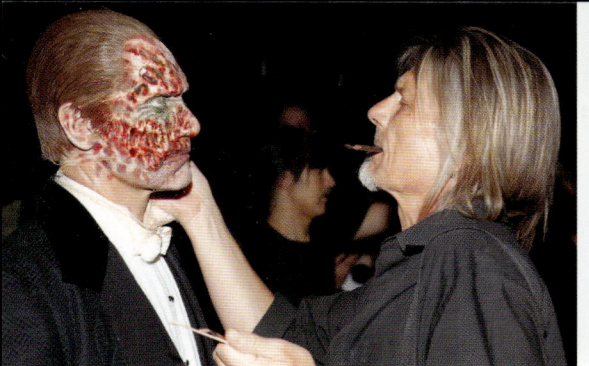

A makeup artist puts makeup on an actor from *The Phantom of the Opera*.

The makeup and costumes in *Chaplin* are black, white, and gray.

Costume designers design the costumes months before a show begins. In *The Lion King*, there are over 250 costumes, and each one is different. The costumes for many big Broadway shows cost as much as $1 million.

Dressers help actors change in and out of costumes during a show. In 2011, in *Baby It's You*, the lead actor changed costumes about 20 times!

Makeup artists do actors' hair and makeup to make them look like their characters.[14] It takes the makeup artist up to two hours to make the lead actor look like the phantom in *Phantom of the Opera*. In the 2012 play *Chaplin*, the makeup artist uses black, white, and gray makeup to make the actors look like they are in a black-and-white movie. The costumes are also black, white, and gray.

[14] **character:** a person in a book, movie, or play

?

EVALUATE

Why do you think actors change costumes during a show?

CHAPTER 4

Show Tunes

SONGS MAKE MUSICALS COME TO LIFE ON BROADWAY.

Musicals are some of the most popular Broadway plays. Musicals use songs to tell part or all of the story. There are many **composers** and **lyricists** who became famous for making music for Broadway shows. Andrew Lloyd Webber has **composed** the music for about 20 musicals, including *Phantom of the Opera* and *Cats*. He started writing the music for *Cats* in 1977, using words from poems by T. S. Eliot. It was on Broadway from 1982 to 2000. The songs have been translated[15] into ten languages.

Richard Rodgers and Oscar Hammerstein worked together to create music. Rodgers composed the music and Hammerstein wrote the **lyrics**. Many of their musicals from the 1940s and 1950s are still popular on Broadway today, and some, like *The Sound of Music*, became successful movies.

[15] **translate:** change from one language to another

Many famous pop musicians have written songs for Broadway musicals. Many older people may know Elton John from his pop songs from the 1970s and 1980s, but younger people may know him better as the composer of Broadway musicals, like *Aida* and *The Lion King*. Singer Bono and guitar player The Edge, from the popular band U2, composed the music and wrote the lyrics for the songs in *Spider-Man: Turn Off the Dark*.

Other musicals take songs that already exist and make a play with them. For *Movin' Out*, on Broadway from 2002 to 2005, choreographer and director Twyla Tharp put Billy Joel's songs together to create a story. In 2001, the band ABBA worked with writer Catherine Johnson to make the musical *Mamma Mia!* with some of ABBA's popular songs, and the band Green Day turned their album[16] *American Idiot* into a musical in 2010.

In *American Idiot*, some actors play guitars on stage.

....
[16] **album:** a group of songs on a CD, etc.

?

ANALYZE

Why do you think musicals use popular musicians to write songs?

Musicians watch the conductor when they play live music.

Audiences love musicals because of the singing and the dancing. But for actors, musicals can be more difficult than other plays because they have to sing, dance, and act. Actors that can do all three well are often called "a triple threat"[17] because they can usually get a part on Broadway more easily than others.

Musicals also have live music. The musicians often sit in front of the stage. However, in *Spider-Man: Turn Off the Dark*, 18 musicians play music in two different rooms below the stage. The music comes through speakers on the stage. The musicians watch the conductor and the actors on video screens.

[17] **triple threat:** something that is three times more dangerous than something else

Toby liked the flying scenes in *Spider-Man* more than the music, but many people go to musicals for the songs. Sometimes there is a song, or show tune, from a play that people remember, and it becomes popular with people who haven't seen the musical.

Musicians recording a song

Ethel Mermen, famous in Broadway musicals in the 1940s, made the song *There's No Business Like Show Business* popular on the radio. Songs from *West Side Story* were popular in the late 1950s and early 1960s. In the late 1970s and early 1980s many children knew the words to *Tomorrow* from the musical *Annie*, and adults listened to Andrew Lloyd Webber's *Don't Cry for Me, Argentina* from *Evita*. In 1994, Elton John recorded *The Circle of Life* from *The Lion King*, and it was one of the top ten pop songs in many countries.

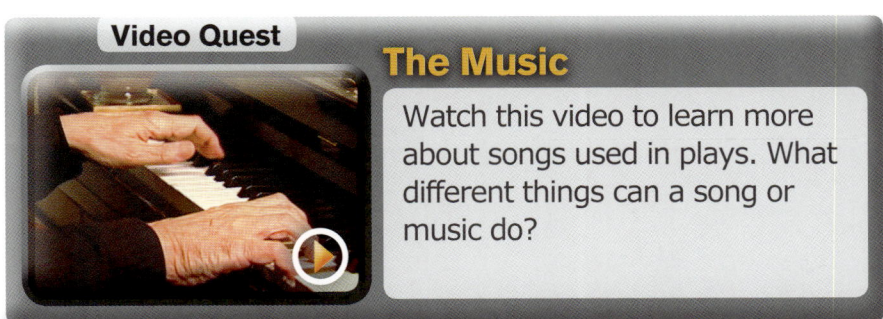

Video Quest

The Music

Watch this video to learn more about songs used in plays. What different things can a song or music do?

CHAPTER 5

On the Road

BROADWAY SHOWS TRAVEL AROUND THE USA AND AROUND THE WORLD.

Producers spend a lot of money to make Broadway shows. A show can cost anywhere from $3 – 20 million. Producers make some money back by selling tickets. A Broadway ticket usually costs between $100 and $300. Producers also make money through merchandising – selling merchandise.

Most Broadway shows have a gift shop in the theater where people can buy things, like cups, toys, music CDs, bags, and clothes. Toby got a *Spider-Man* T-shirt when he saw the play. Many people buy souvenirs[18] in the gift shops for family and friends.

People can buy merchandise from a Broadway show even if they don't go to actually see the play.

[18] **souvenir:** something you buy to remember something special

This is because most shows have online stores. Between 1,400 and 2,000 T-shirts from the musical *Spamalot* are sold every week. People can also buy and download music online from Broadway musicals.

Producers also make a lot of money by taking Broadway shows on the road. Toby went to New York City to see *Spider-Man*, but he can see many Broadway shows where he lives in Michigan.

Producers often take a Broadway show to different cities, and it plays for a few weeks in each place. They sell a lot of tickets and a lot of merchandise, too. Some shows even travel around the world. In addition to cities in the USA and England, *The Phantom of the Opera* played in several other cities around the world. It went to Tokyo, Japan, Johannesburg in South Africa, and Budapest, Hungary.

Phantom of the Opera was popular in Tokyo.

New costumes, sets, and props are needed for traveling Broadway shows. The stages can be smaller in different places, so sometimes the set is different. Set designers often make props lighter, so it is easier to travel with them. For *The Lion King*, they use 20 big trucks to take the set, costumes, and props to different cities.

Many shows travel while they are still on Broadway, so different actors are in the traveling shows.

Stagehands and other behind-the-scenes workers usually don't go on the road. Shows often hire[19] stagehands in different cities, and actors sometimes do their own hair and makeup. For *The Lion King*, producers hire 60 to 80 people in each city to get the set ready, and they hire about 35 people to work during the show.

[19] **hire:** give someone a job

An actor in the traveling show
The Lion King

Shrek was more popular in London than in New York City.

Many Broadway shows start in other cities. It is expensive to hire actors, stagehands, and other people and to rent[20] a theater in New York City. So, some shows start in other cities because it is cheaper. For example, *Phantom of the Opera* started in London before it came to Broadway. If a show doesn't do well in another city first, it may not make it to Broadway. If a show is successful, it comes to Broadway.

Sometimes, the opposite happens. A show flops on Broadway but is successful in another city. *Shrek the Musical* didn't do well on Broadway. The producers took the show to London. It was more popular there, so the producers made more money selling tickets. Also, it cost $640,000 a week to run *Shrek* in New York City but only about half of that in London.

[20] **rent:** pay money to use or live in a building that someone else owns

UNDERSTAND

How is a traveling Broadway show different from a show on Broadway in New York City?

CHAPTER 6

What Do You Think?

IMAGINE THAT YOU WORK ON BROADWAY.

There are many jobs for people on Broadway. Read about what these people do for a Broadway musical.

Name	Position	Job Description
Paula	Writer	Writes the story for the play
Shawn	Composer and Lyricist	Writes the music and the lyrics for the songs in the play
Marcia	Choreographer	Creates all of the dances for the show
Marcos	Set Designer	Creates the idea for the set
Jon	Carpenter	Builds walls and furniture for the set
Sylvia	Costume Designer	Designs all of the costumes for the play
Brian	Lighting Designer	Creates the lighting for the play
Jennifer	Actor	Plays the main part Acts, sings, dances
Lyle	Stagehand	Brings scenery on stage during the show
Lin	Makeup Artist	Does hair and makeup for five actors
Brittany	Dresser	Helps 10 actors get into their costumes
Wendy	Musician	Plays the guitar
Ahmed	Sound Engineer	Operates the sound effects during the show

Which job do you think is the most difficult? Which job would you like to do? Why? Which job wouldn't you like to have? Why not?

Imagine you are going to create a new musical. Choose one of these ideas for the story or think of your own idea.

A musical about . . .

- your favorite book
- your favorite band
- your life
- a famous person in history
- an interesting city
- an imaginary place
- characters in a TV show
- an important moment in history

What are your plans for the play? What does the set look like? What music are you using? Who is playing the main parts? What merchandise do you sell?

After You Read

Read the sentences and choose Ⓐ (True) or Ⓑ (False).
If the book does not tell you, choose Ⓒ.

1 The first big theater was built in New York City in 1750.
- Ⓐ True
- Ⓑ False
- Ⓒ Doesn't say

2 A play doesn't have to be on the street Broadway to be a Broadway show.
- Ⓐ True
- Ⓑ False
- Ⓒ Doesn't say

3 All actors have to go to auditions to get a part on Broadway.
- Ⓐ True
- Ⓑ False
- Ⓒ Doesn't say

4 Stagehands only work backstage.
- Ⓐ True
- Ⓑ False
- Ⓒ Doesn't say

Video
5 The sound designer only works with music.
- Ⓐ True
- Ⓑ False
- Ⓒ Doesn't say

6 Musicals with songs by pop musicians are the most popular musicals.
- Ⓐ True
- Ⓑ False
- Ⓒ Doesn't say

Answer the Questions

Answer the questions with the names of jobs. More than one answer is possible.

1 Who is on stage during a play?

_____

2 Who helps actors rehearse?

_____

3 Who works backstage during a show?

_____

4 Who designs things for a play?

_____

5 Who builds the sets?

_____

6 Who works with the props?

_____

Text Completion

Complete the advertisement with the words from the box.

backdrops	costumes	merchandise	musical	props	sets

A new Broadway **1** _____ is coming to Miami.
We need you!

We are looking for . . .

- carpenters to build **2** _____.
- artists to paint **3** _____.
- stagehands to move **4** _____.
- dressers to help actors change **5** _____.
- people to sell **6** _____.

Answer Key

Words to Know, page 4
① part **②** musical **③** audience **④** scene **⑤** scenery **⑥** set

Words to Know, page 5
① costume **②** merchandise **③** prop **④** backstage
⑤ backdrop

Analyze, page 7 *Answers will vary.*

Video Quest, page 11
Actors rehearse before they go on stage, learn their parts, and practice together. They work with the director to practice the words, the songs, and how move on stage.

Video Quest, page 13 *Answers will vary.*

Evaluate, page 15 *Answers will vary.*

Analyze, page 17 *Answers will vary.*

Video Quest, page 19 *Answers will vary.*

Understand, page 23 *Answers will vary.*

True or False?, page 26
① A **②** A **③** B **④** B **⑤** B **⑥** C

Answer the Questions, page 27
① actors, stagehands **②** directors, choreographers, coaches **③** stagehands, dressers **④** set designers, costume designers, lighting designers, sound designers **⑤** carpenters **⑥** actors, stagehands, carpenters

Text Completion, page 27
① musical **②** sets **③** backdrops **④** props **⑤** costumes
⑥ merchandise